A Most Pleasant Comedy Of Mucedorus The Kings Sonne Of Valentia, And Amadine The Kings Daughter Of Arragon

William Shakespeare

In the interest of creating a more extensive selection of rare historical book reprints, we have chosen to reproduce this title even though it may possibly have occasional imperfections such as missing and blurred pages, missing text, poor pictures, markings, dark backgrounds and other reproduction issues beyond our control. Because this work is culturally important, we have made it available as a part of our commitment to protecting, preserving and promoting the world's literature. Thank you for your understanding.

Mucedorus

A Most pleasant Comedie of Muce-
dorus the Kings sonne of *Valentia*, and *Amadine* the Kinges daughter of *Aragon*.

With the merry conceites of *Mouse*.

Amplified with new additions, as it was acted before the Kings Maiestie at White-hall on Shroue-sunday night.

By his Highnes Seruantes vsually playing at the Globe.

Very delectable, and full of conceited Mirth.

Imprinted at London for *William Iones*, dwelling neare Holborne Conduit at the signe of the Gunne.
1610.

The Prologue.

MOst sacred Maiestie, whose great desertes,
Thy Subiect *England*; nay, the World admires:
Which, Heauen graunt still increase; O may your Prayse
Multiplying with your houres, your Fame still rayse:
Embrace your Counsell; Loue, with Fayth, them guide:
That both as one bench, by each others side,
So may your life passe on, and runne so euen,
That your firme zeale, plant you a Throne in Heauen:
Where smiling Angels shall your guardians bee
From blemisht Traytors, stayn'd with Periurie:
And as the night's inferiour to the day,
So be all earthly Regions, to your sway.
Be as the Sunne to Day, the Day to Night;
For, from your Beames, *Europe* shall borrow light.
Mirth drowne your boosome, faire Delight your minde,
And may our Pastime, your Contentment finde.

Exit.

A ii.

Ten persons may esily
play it.

The King, and Rombelo, } for one.

King Valencia, } for one.

Mucedorus the Prince of Valencia, } for one.

Anselmo, } for one.

Amadine the Kings daughter of Aragon, } for one.

Segasto a Noble man, } for one.

Enuie, Tremelio a Captaine, Bremo a wild man. } for one.

Comedie, a Boy, an old woman, Ariena, Amadines mayde, } for one.

Collin a Counseller, a Messenger, } for one.

Mouse the Clowne, } for one.

A most pleasant Comedie of

Mucedorus the Kinges Sonne of *Valencia*, and
Amadine the Kings Daughter of *Aragon*.

Enter Comedie ioyfully, with a Garland of Bayes on her head.

Hy so; thus doe I hope to please:
Musicke reuiues, and Mirth is tollerable;
Comedie play thy part, and please:
Make merry them that comes to ioy with thee
Ioy the good gentles, I hope to make you laugh
Sound foorth *Bellonas* siluer tuned stringes,
Time sittes vs well, the day and place is ours.

Enter Enuie his armes naked besmeared with blood.

En. Nay stay Minion, there lies a blocke:
What, all on mirth, Ile interrupt your tale,
And mixe your Musicke with a tragicke end.

Com. What monstrous vgly Hagge is this,
That dares controule the pleasures of our will?
Vaunt churlish curre, besmeard with gorie blood,
That seemst to check the blossom of delight,
And stiffe the sound of sweete *Bellonas* bearth.
Blush monster, blush, and poste away with shame,
That seekest disturbance of a Goddesse deeds.

En. Post hence thy selfe, thou counterchecking trull,
I will possesse this habite spight of thee,
And gaine the glory of thy wished port:
Ile thunder Musicke shall apale the Nymphes,
And make them shiuer their clattering strings,
Flying for succour to their Danish caues.

Sound Drummes within, and cry stab, stab.

Hearken, thou shalt heare a noyse,
Shall fill the ayre with a shrilling sound,

A 3.   And

The Comedie

And thunder Musicke to Gods aboue:
Mars shall himsefe breath downe
A peerelesse Crowne vpon braue *Envies* head,
And raise his chiuall with a lasting fame:
In this braue Musicke *Enuy* takes delight,
Where I may see them wallow in their blood,
To spurne at Armes and Legges quite shiuered off,
And heare the cryes of many thousand slaine:
How lik'st thou this my trull? thi's sport alone for me.

Co. Vaunt bloody curre, nurst vp with Tygers sap,
That so dost quaile a Womans minde;
Comedie is milde, gentle, willing for to please,
And seekes to gaine the loue of all estates:
Delighting in Mirth, mixt all with louely tales,
And bringeth thinges with treble ioy to passe:
Thou bloody, enuious, disdayner of mens ioyes,
Whose name is fraught with bloody stratagems,
Delights in nothing but in spoyle and death,
Where thou mayst trample in their luke-warme blood,
And graspe their hearts within thy cursed pawes:
Yet vaile thy minde, reuenge thou not on mee,
A silly Woman begges it at thy hands:
Giue me the leaue to vtter out my Play;
Forbeare this place, I humbly craue thee hence,
And mixe not Death mongst pleasing Comedies,
That treates nought else but pleasure and delight:
If any sparke of humaine rests in thee,
Forbeare, be gone, tender the suite of mee.

En. Why so I will, forbeare shall be such,
As treble death shall crosse thee with despight,
And make thee mourne where most thou ioyest,
Turning thy mirth into a deadly dole:
Whirling thy pleasures with a peale of death,
And drench thy methods in a sea of Blood:
This will I doe? thus shall I beare with thee:
And more, to vexe thee with a deeper spight,
I will with threats of blood begin thy Play,
Fauouring thee with Enuie and with Hate,

of Mucedorus.

Com. Then vgly Monster, doe thy worst,
I will defend them in despight of thee:
And though thou thinkst with tragicke fumes
To praue my Play vnto my deepe disgrace,
I forceit not, I scorne what thou canst doe:
Ile grace it so, thy selfe shall it confesse,
From Tragicke stuffe, to be a pleasant Comedie.

En. Why then *Comedie*, send thy Actors foorth,
And I will crosse the first steppes of their trade,
Making them feare the very dart of Death.

Com. And Ile defend them maugre all thy spight:
So vgly Fiend farewell, till time shall serue,
That we may meete to parle for the best.

En. Content *Comedie*, Ile goe spread my branch,
And scattered blossomes from mine inuious Tree,
Shall prooue two Monsters, spoyling of their ioyes.   *Exit.*

Sound.   Enter *Mucedorus* and *Ansel his friend.*
Muced. Anselmo.   *Ansel.* My Lord and friend.

Muc. True my *Anselmo*, both thy Lord and friend
Whose deare affections boosome with my heart,
And keepe their domination in one orbe.

Ans. Whence neare disloyaltie shall roote it foorth,
But fayth plant firmer in your choyse respect.

Muc. Much blame were mine, if I should other deeme,
Nor can coy Fortune contrary allow:
But my *Anselmo*, loth I am to say, I must estrange that frendship,
Misconsture not, tis from the Realme, not thee:
Though Landes part Bodies, Heartes keepe companie;
Thou knowst that I imparted often haue,
Priuate relations with my royall Sire
Had, as concerning beautious *Amadine*,
Rich *Aragons* bright Iewell; whose face (some say)
That blooming Lillies neuer shone so gay,
Excelling, not exceld: yet least Report
Does mangle Veritie, boasting of what is not,
Wing'd with Desire; thither Ile straight repaire,
And be my Fortunes as my Thoughts are, faire.

Ans. Will you forsake *Valencia*, leaue the Court,

Absent

The Comedie

Absent you from the eye of Soueraigntie,
Do not sweete Prince, aduenture on that taske,
Since danger lurkes each where, be wonne from it.

Mu. Desist dissuasion,
My resolution brookes no batterie,
Therefore if thou retaine thy wonted forme,
Assist what I intend.

Ans. Your misse will breed a blemish in the Court,
And throw a frostie deaw vpon that Beard,
Whose front *Valencia* stoopes to.

Mu. If thou my welfare tender, then no more,
Let Loues strong Magicke, charme thy triuiail phrase,
Wasted as vainely, as to gripe the Sunne:
Augment not then more answers; locke thy lippes,
Vnlesse thy wisedome suite me with disguise,
According to my purpose.

Ans. That action craues no counsell,
Since what you rightly are, will more commaund,
Then best vsurped shape.

Mu. Thou still art opposite in disposition,
A more obscure seruile habillament
Beseemes this enterprise.

Ans. Then like a *Florentine* or *Mountebancke*.

Mu. Tis much too tedious, I dislike thy iudgement,
My minde is grafted on an humbler stocke.

Ans. Within my Closet does there hang a Cassocke,
Though base the weede is, t'was a Shepheards,
Which I presented in Lord *Iulios* Maske.

Mu. That my *Anselmo*, and none else but that,
Maske *Mucedorus* from the vulgar view,
That habite suites my minde; fetch me that weede.

Exit Anselmo.

Better then Kinges, haue not disdaind that state,
And much inferiour, to obtaine their mate.

Enter Anselmo with a Shepheards coate.

So, let our respect commaund thy secrecie,
At once a briefe farewell,
Delay to louers, is a second hell.

Exit Mucedorus, Anselmo.

of Macedorus.

Ans. Prosperitie forerunne thee, Awkward chance
Neuer be neighbour to thy wishes venture:
Content and Fame aduance thee, euer thriue,
And Glory thy mortalitie suruiue. *Exit.*

Enter Mouse with a bottle of Hay.

Mouse. O horrible terrible! Was euer poore Gentleman so scard out of his seauen Senses? A Beare? nay sure it cannot be a Beare; but some Diuell in a Beares Doublet: for a Beare could neuer haue had that agilitie, to haue frighted me: Well, Ile see my Father hang'd, before Ile serue his Horse any more: Well, Ile carry home my Bottle of Hay, and for once, make my Fathers Horse turne Puritane and obserue Fasting dayes; for he gets not a bit. But soft, this way she followed me, therefore Ile take the other Path; and because Ile be sure to haue an eye on him, I will take handes with some foolish Creditor, and make euery step backward.

As he goes backwards the Beare comes in, and he tumbles ouer her, and runnes e way, and leaues his bottle of Hay behind him.

Enter Segasto running, and Amadine after him, being pursued with a Beare.

Seg. Oh flie Madame, flie, or else we are but dead.

Am. Helpe *Segasto*, helpe, helpe sweete *Segasto*, or else I die.

Segasto runnes away.

Seg. Alasse Madame, there is no way but flight,
Then haste and saue your selfe.

Am. Why then I die: Ah helpe me in distresse.

Enter Macedorus like a Shepheard, with a sword drawne, and a Beares head in his hand.

Mac. Stay Lady stay, and be no more dismayde,
That cruell Beast, most mercilesse and fell,
Which hath bereaued thousapds of their liues:
Affrighted many with his hard pursues,
Prying from place to place to find his Prey,
Prolonging thus his life by others death,
His Carcasse now lies headlesse voyde of breath.

Am. That foule deformed Monster, is he dead?

Mac. Assure your selfe thereof, behold his head:

B.   Which

The Comedie

Which if it please you Lady, to accept,
With willing heart I yeeld it to your Maiestie.
　Am. Thankes worthy Shepheard thankes a thousand times,
This gift assure thy selfe contentes me more
Then greatest bountie of a mightie Prince,
Although he were the monarch of the world.
　Mu. Most gratious Goddesse, more then mortall wight,
Your heauenly hue of right importes no lesse:
Most glad am I, in that it was my chance,
To vndertake this enterprise in hand,
Which doth so greatly glad your Princely minde.
　Am. No Goddesse Shepheard, but a mortall wight,
A mortall wight distressed as thou seest:
My Father heere is King of *Arragon*,
I, *Amadine* his onely daughter am:
And after him, sole heire vnto the Crowne:
Now whereas it is my Fathers will
To marrie me vnto *Segasto*,
On whose wealth, through Fathers former vsurie,
Is knowne to be no lesse then wonderfull:
We both of custome often times did vse
(Leauing the Court) to walke within the fields
For recreation, especially the Spring,
In that it yeelds great store of rare delights:
And passing further then our wonted walkes:
Scarse entred were within these lucklesse Woods,
But right before vs downe a steepe-fall hill,
A monstrous vgly Beare did hie him fast
To meete vs both: I faint to tell the rest.
Good shepheard, but suppose the gastly lookes,
The hideous feares, the thousand hundred woes,
Which at this instant *Amadine* sustaind.
　Mu. Yet worthy Princesse let thy sorrow cease,
And let this sight your former ioyes reuiue.
　Am. Beleeue me Shepheard, so it doth no lesse.
　Mu. Long may they last vnto your heartes content.
But tell me Lady, what is become of him
Segasto cald? what is become of him?

Am.

of Mucedorus.

Am. I know not I, that know the powers diuine:
But God graunt this, that sweete *Segasto* liue.
  Mu. Yet hard hearted he in such a case,
So cowardly to saue himselfe by flight,
And leaue so braue a Princesse to the spoyle.
  Am. Well Shepheard, for thy worthy valour tried,
Endangering thy selfe to set me free,
Vnrecompensed sure thou shalt not be:
In Court thy courage shall be plainely knowne,
Throughout the Kingdome will I spread thy name,
To thy renowne and neuer dying fame:
And that thy courage may be better knowne,
Beare thou the Head of this most monstrous Beast,
In open sight, to euery Courtiers view:
So will the King my Father thee reward.
Come lets away, and guard me to the Court.
  Mu. With all my heart.   *Exeunt.*
        Enter Segasto solus.
  Seg. When heapes of harmes do houer ouer head,
Tis time as then (some say) to looke about,
And so insuing harmes to chuse the least:
But hard, yea haplesse is that wretches chance,
Lucklesse his lot, and Caytiue-like accurst,
At whose proceedings Fortune euer frownes:
My selfe I meane, most subiect vnto thrall:
For I, the more I seeke to shunne the worst,
The more by proofe I find my selfe accurst.
Ere-whiles assaulted with an vgly Beare,
Faire *Amadine* in company all alone:
Foorthwith by flight I thought to saue my selfe,
Leauing my *Amadine* vnto her shiftes:
For death it was for to resist the Beare,
And death no lesse, of *Amadines* harmes to heare.
Accursed I, in lingring life thus long,
In liuing thus, each minute of an houre
Doth pierce my heart with dartes of thousand deaths:
If she by flight, her furie doe escape,
What will she thinke?

Will

The Comedie

Will she not say, yea flatly to my face,
Accusing me of meere disloyaltie,
A trustie friend is tride in time of neede?
But I, when she in danger was of death,
And needed me, and cried, *Segasto* helpe:
I turnd my backe and quickly ranne away,
Vnworthie I to beare this vitall breath:
But what; what needs these plaints?
If *Amadine* do liue, then happie I,
She will in time forgiue and so forget:
Amadine is mercifull, not *Iuno* like,
In harmefull heart to harbor hatred long.

Enter Mouse the Clowne runing crying Clubs.

Mou. Clubs, Prongs Pitchforkes, Billes: Oh helpe,
A Beare, a Beare, a Beare.

Seg. Still Beares, and nothing els but beares:
Tell me sirra where she is.

Clow. O sir she is runne downe the woods,
I saw her white head and her white belly.

Seg. Thou talkest of wonders, to tell me of white Beares,
But sirra, didst thou euer see any such?

Clo. No faith, I neuer saw any such,
But I remember my Fathers words,
He bad me take heed I was not caught with a white Beare.

Seg. A lamentable tale no doubt.

Clo. I tell you what sir, as I was going afielde to serue my fathers great Horse, and arried a bottle of hay vpon my head: now do you see sir, I fast hudwinckt, that I could see nothing, I perceiuing the Beare comming, I threw my hay into the hedge, and ran away.

Seg. What, from nothing?

Clo. I warrant you yes, I saw some thing: for there was two load of Thornes, besides my bottle of hay, and that made three.

Seg. But tell me sirra: the Beare that thou didst see,
Did she not beare a bucket on her arme?

Col. Ha, ha, ha,: I neuer saw Beare go a milking in all my life,
But harke you sir: I did not looke so high as her arme,
I saw nothing but her white head, and her white belly.

Seg.

Seg. But tell me sirra: Where dost thou dwell?
Col. Why, do you not know me?
Seg. Why no, how should I know thee?
Col. Why then you know no body and you know not me:
I'tell you sir, I am the good-man Rats Sonne of the next Parish
ouer the hill.
Seg. Good-man Rats sonne: Why what's thy name?
Clo. Why I am very neere kin vnto him.
Seg. I thinke so, but what's thy name.
Clo. My name: I haue a very prettie name: Ile tell you what
my name is: my name is *Mouse.*
Seg. What plaine *Mouse.*
Clo. I plaine Mouse without either welt or gard:
But do you heare sir, I am but a very young *Mouse*, for my taile
is scarse growne out yet: looke you here else.
Seg. But I pray thee who gaue thee that name?
Clo. Faith sir I know not that, but if you would faine know,
aske my fathers great Horse, for he hath been halfe a yeare longer
with my Father then I haue.
Seg. This seemes to be a merrie fellow,
I care not if I take him home with me:
Mirth is a comfort to a troubled minde,
A merrie Man, a merrie Maister makes.
How sayst thou sirra, wilt thou dwell with me?
Clo. Nay soft sir, two wordes to a bargaine: pray you, what
occupation are you?
Seg. No occupation, I liue vpon my Landes.
Clo. Your Lands? away, you are no Maister for me: Why do
you thinke that I am so mad, to go seeke my liuing in the Lands
amongst the Stones, Bryers, and Bushes, and teare my Holy-
day apparell: not I by your leaue.
Seg. Why, I do not meane thou shalt.   *Clo.* How then?
Seg. Why thou shalt be my man, and waite vpon me at the
Clo. What's that?   *Seg.* Where the King lies.   (Court.
Clo. What's that same King, a man or a woman?
Seg. A man as thou art.
Clo. As I am: harke you sir, pray you what kin is he to good-
man King of our parish, the Churchwarden?

B 3.   *Seg.*

The Comedie

Seg. No kin to him, he is the King of the whole land.
Clo. King of the land, I neuer see him.
Seg. If thou wilt dwel with me, thou shalt see him euery day.
Clo. Shall I go home againe to be torne in peeces with Bears? No not I : I will goe home and put on a cleane Shirt, and then goe drowne my selfe.
Seg. Thou shalt not need, if thou wilt dwell with mee, thou shalt want nothing.
Clo. Shall I not ? then heer's my hand, Ile dwell with you : And harke you sir, now you haue entertained me, I will tell you what I can do: I can keepe my Tongue from picking and stealing, and my Hands from lying and slaundering, I warrant you, as well as euer you had Man in all your life.
Seg. Now will I to Court with sorrowfull heart rounded with doubts ; if *Amadine* do liue, then happy I : yea happie I, if *Amadine* do liue.

Enter the King with a young Prince Prisoner, Amadine, Tremelio, with Collin and Counsellers.

King. Now braue Lords, our Warres are brought to end,
Our foes the foyle, and we in safety rest :
It ys behooues to vse such clemency in peace,
As valour in the warres :
It is as greate honour to be bountifull at home,
As to be Conquerors in the field :
Therefore my Lords, the more to my content,
Your liking, and your Countries safegard,
We are dispos'd in marriage for to giue
Our Daughter to Lord *Segasto* heere,
Who shall succeede the Diademe after mee,
And raigne hereafter as I tofore haue done,
Your sole and lawfull King of *Arragon*,
What say you Lordings, like you of my aduice?
Col. An't please your Maiesty, we do not only allow of your Highnes pleasure, but also vow faithfully in what we may to further it.
King. Thankes good my Lords, if long *Adrastus* liue,
He will at full requite your curtesies.
Tremelio, in recompence of thy late valour done,

Take

of Macedorus.

Take vnto thee the *Catalone*, a Prince
Lately our Prisoner taken in the Warres:
Be thou his Keeper, his ransome shall be thine,
Wee'le thinke of it when leasure shall affoord:
Meane while do vse him well, his father is a King.

Tre. Thankes to your Maiesty, his vsage shall be such
As he thereat shall thinke no cause to grutch. *Exeunt.*

King. Then march we on to Court, & rest our wearied limbs.
But *Collin*, I haue a tale in secret kept for thee,
When thou shalt heare a watch-word from thy King,
Thinke then, some waighty matter is at hand,
That highly shall concerne our State:
Then *Collin*, looke thou be not farre from me:
And for the seruice thou tofore hast done,
Thy truth, and valour proou'd in euery point,
I shall with bounties thee inlarge therefore:
So guard vs to the Court.

Col. What so my Soueraigne doth commaund me doe,
With willing minde I gladly yeeld consent. *Exeunt.*

Enter Segasto and the Clowne with Weapons about him.

Seg. Tell me sirra, How do you like your Weapons?

Clo. O very well, very well, they keepe my sides warme.

Seg. They keep the dogs frō your shins very wel, do they not

Clo. How? keep the dogs from my shins, I would scorne but
my shins could keepe the dogs from them.

Seg. Well sirra, leauing idle talke, tell mee,
Doest thou know Captaine *Tremelios* Chamber?

Clo. I very well, it hath a doore.

Seg. I thinke so, for so hath euery Chamber:
But doest thou know the man?

Clo. I forsooth, he hath a nose on his face.

Seg. Why so hath euery one. *Clo.* That's more then I know.

Seg. But dost thou remember the Captaine that was here with
the King euen now, that brought the young Prince Prisoner?

Clo. O very well.

Seg. Gue vnto him, and bid him come vnto mee:
Tell him I haue a matter in secret to impart to him.

Clo. I will Maister. Maister whats his name?

Seg.

Seg. Why, Captaine *Tremelio.*
Clo. O the Mealeman; I know him very well,
He bringes Meale euery Saterday: But harke you Maister;
Must I bid him come to you, or must you come to him?
　Seg. No sirra, he must come to me.
　Clo. Harke you Maister; how if he be not at home,
What shall I doe then?
　Seg. Why then leaue word with some of his folkes.
　Clo. O Maister, if there be no body within,
I will leaue word with his Dogge.
　Seg. Why, can his Dogge speake?
　Clo. I cannot tell; wherfore doth he keepe his Chamber else?
　Seg. To keepe out such knaues as thou art.
　Clo. Nay by Lady; then goe your selfe.
　Seg. You will goe sir, will you not?
　Clo. Yes marie will I : O tis come to my head :
And a bee not within, Ile bring his Chamber to you.
　Seg. What, wilt thou plucke downe the Kinges House?
　Clo. Nay by Lady, Ile know the price of it first.
Maister, it is such a hard name, I haue forgotten it againe:
I pray you tell me his name?
　Seg. I tell thee, Captaine *Tremelio.*
　Clo. Oh Captaine treble knaue, Captaine treble knaue.
　　　　　Enter Tremelio.
　Tre. How now sirra, dost thou call me?
　Clo. You must come to my Maister, Captaine Treble knaue.
　Tre. My Lord *Segasto*, did you send for me?
　Seg. I did *Tremelio* : Sirra, about your businesse.
　Clo. I mary, Whats that, can you tell?
　Seg. No not well.
　Clo. Marie then I can; straight to the Kitchin-dresser to *Iohn* the Cooke, and get mee a good peece of Beefe and Brewis, and then to the Butterie hatch to *Thomas* the Butler, for a Iacke of Beere; and there, for an houre Ile so belabour my selfe : and therefore I pray you call me not till you thinke I haue done, I pray you good Maister. *Exit.*
　Seg. Well sir, away.
Tremelio, this it is; thou knowest the valour of *Segasto*,
　　　　　　　　　　　　　　　　　　　Spread

of Mucedorus.

Spread through all the Kingdome of *Aragon*,
And such as haue found triumph and fauours:
Neuer daunted at any time: But now a Shepheard,
Admired at in Court for Worthinesse,
And *Segasto's* honour layd aside:
My will therefore is this, that thou doest finde some meanes to
worke the Shepheards death: I know thy strength sufficient to
performe my desire, and thy loue no otherwise then to reuenge
my iniuries.

Tre. It is not the frownes of a Shepheard that *Tremelio* feares:
Therefore account it accomplish'd what I take in hand.

Seg. Thankes good *Tremelio*, and assure thy selfe,
What I promise that I will performe.

Tre. Thankes good my Lord: And in good time,
See where he commeth, stand by a while,
And you shall see me put in practise your intended drift:
Haue at thee Swaine if that I hit thee right.

Enter Mucedorus.

Mu. Vilde coward, so without cause to strike a man,
Turne coward turne, now strike and do thy worst.

Mucedorus killeth him.

Seg. Hold Shepheard hold, spare him kill him not,
Accursed villaine, tell me, What hast thou done?
Ah *Tremelio* trustie *Tremelio*, I sorrow for thy death,
And since that thou liuing didst prooue faithfull to
Segasto, so *Segasto* now liuing will honour the dead
Corpes of *Tremelio* with reuenge.
Bloud thirstie villaine, borne and bred in mercilesse murther,
Tell me, how durst thou be so bold,
As once to lay thy handes vpon the least of mine?
Assure thy selfe thou shalt be vsde according to the law.

Mu. *Segasto* cease, these threates are needelesse,
Accuse me not of murther, that haue done nothing
But in mine owne defence.

Seg. Nay Shepheard reason not with me,
Ile manifest thy fact vnto the King:
Whose doome will be thy death as thou deseru'st,
What hoe, *Mouse*, come away.

C.   *Clo.*

The Comedie
Enter Mouse.

Clo. Why how now, what's the matter?
I thought you would be calling before I had done.
  Seg. Come helpe away with my friend.
  Clo. Why is he drunke? cannot he stand on his feete?
  Seg. No, he is not drunke, he is slaine.
  Clo. Slaine? no by Lady he is not slaine.
  Seg. Hee's kild I tell thee.   (longer.
  Clo. What do you vse to kill your friends? I wil serue you no
  Seg. I tell thee, the Shepheard kild him.
  Clo. O did a so: but Maister, I will haue all his apparrell if I
carry him away.   Seg. Why so thou shalt.
  Clo. Come then, I will helpe: mas Maister I thinke his Mother sung Looby to him, he is so heauie.   *Exeunt.*
  Mu. Behold the fickle state of man, alwayes mutable, neuer at one.
Sometimes we feede on fancies with the sweete of our desires:
Sometimes againe, we feele the heate of extreame miseries.
Now am I in fauour about the Court and Countrey;
To morrow those fauours will turne to frownes,
To day I liue reuenged on my foe,
To morrow I die, my foe reuenged on me.   *Exit.*

Enter Bremo a wilde man.
  Bre. No passenger this morning? what not one?
A chance that seldome doth befall.
What not one? then ly thou there,
And rest thy selfe till I haue further need:
Now *Bremo*, sith thy leasure so affoords,
An endlesse thing, who knowes not *Bremoes* strength:
Who like a King commander within these woods,
The Beare, the Boare, dares not abide my sight,
But haste away to saue themselues by flight:
The christall waters in the bubling Brookes,
When I come by, doth swiftly slide away.
And claps themselues in closets vnder bankes,
Afraide to looke bold *Bremo* in the face:
The aged Oakes at *Bremoes* breath doth bowe,
And all thinges else are still at my commaund.

Else

of Mucedorus.

Else what would I?
Rend them in peeces, and plucke them from the earth,
And each way else I would reuenge my selfe.
Why who comes heere, with whom I dare not fight,
Who fights with me and doth not dy the death? not one,
What fauour shewes this sturdie sticke to those
That here within these Woodes are combatants with mee?
Why Death, and nothing else but present death,
With restlesse Rage, I wander through these Woods:
No creature heere, but feareth *Bremos* force,
Man, Woman, Child, Beast and Bird,
And euery thing that doth approch my sight,
Are forc't to fall, if *Bremo* once doe frowne.
Come Cudgell come, my partner in my spoyles,
For here I see this day it will not be:
But when it fals that I encounter any,
One patte suffizeth for to worke my will.
What, comes not one? then lets be gone,
A time will serue, when we shall better speed. *Exit.*

Enter the King, Segasto, the Shepheard, and the Clowne, with others.

King. Shepheard, thou hast heard thine accusers,
Murther is layd to thy charge:
What canst thou say? thou hast deserued death.

Mu. Dread Soueraigne, I must needes confesse,
I slue this Captaine in mine owne defence,
Not of any malice, but by chaunce:
But mine accuser hath a further meaning.

Seg. Wordes will not heere preuaile,
I seeke for Iustice; and Iustice craues his death.

Kin. Shepheard, thine owne confussiõ hath condemned thee.
Sirra, take him away, and do him to execution straight.

Clo. So he shall, I warrant him:
But do you heare maister King; he is kinne to a Monkie,
His Necke is bigger then his Head.

Seg. Come sirra, away with him,
And hang him about the middle.

Clo. Yes forsooth I warrant you: Come on sirra:
A, so like a Sheepe-biter a lookes.

C 2. *Enter*

The Comedie

Enter Amadine, and a Boy, with a Beares head.

Am. Dread Soueraigne and wellbeloued Sire;
On bended knee I craue the life of this condemned Shepheard,
which heretofore preserued the life of thy sometime distressed
Daughter

King. Preseru'd the life of my sometime distressed daughter,
How can that be? I neuer knew the time
Wherein thou wast distrest: I neuer knew the day,
But that I haue maintained thy estate,
As best beseem'd the daughter of a King:
I neuer saw the Shepheard vntill now;
How comes it then, that he preseru'd thy life?

Am. Once walking with *Segasto* in the Woods,
Further then our accustomed manner was,
Right before vs downe a steepe-fall hill,
A monstrous vgly Beare did hie him fast
To meete vs both: now whether this be true,
I referre it to the credite of *Segasto*.

Seg. Most true, an't like your Maiestie.   *King.* How then?

Am. The Beare being eager to obtaine his prey,
Made forward to vs with an open mouth,
As if he meant to swallow vs both at once:
The sight whereof did make vs both to dread,
But specially your daughter *Amadine*,
Who for I saw no succour incident,
But in *Segastos* valour, I grew desperate:
And he most coward-like began to flie,
Left me distrest to be deuour'd of him:
How say you *Segasto*, is it not true?

King. His silence verifies it to be true: What then?

Am. Then I amazde, distressed all alone,
Did hie me fast to scape that vgly Beare:
But all in vaine, for why he reached after me,
And hardly I did oft escape his pawes:
Till at the length this Shepheard came,
And brought to me his head.   (Maiesty.
Come hither Boy, Loe heere it is, which I present vnto your

King. The slaughter of this Beare deserues greate fame.

Seg.

of Mucedorus.

Seg. The slaughter of a man, deserues great blame:
King. Indeed occasion often times so fals out.
Seg. Tremelio in the Warres (O King) preserued thee.
Am. The Shepheard in the Woods (O King) preserued mee.
Seg. Tremelio fought when many men did yeeld.
Am. So would the Shepheard, had he beene in field.
Clo. So would my Maister had he not runne away.
Seg. Tremelio's force saued thousands from the foe.
Am. The Shepheards force hath saued thousands moe.
Clo. A ye shipsticks, nothing else.
King. Segasto, cease to accuse the Shepheard,
His worthinesse deserues a recompence:
All we are bound to doe the Shepheard good:
Shepheard, whereas it was my sentence thou shoulst die,
So shall my sentence stand, for thou shalt die.
Seg. Thanks to your Maiestie.
King. But soft Segasto, not for this offence:
Long mayst thou liue, and when the Sisters shall decree,
To cut in twaine the twisted thread of life,
Then let him die; for this, I set him free,
And for thy valour I will honour thee.
Mu. Thanks to your Maieshe.
King. Come daughter, let vs now depart to honor the worthy
valour of the Shepheard with our rewards. *Exeunt.*
Clo. O Maister heare you; you haue made a fresh hand now,
You would bestow you: What will you do now?
You haue lost me a good occupation by the meanes:
Faith Maister, now I cannot hang the Shepheard,
I pray you let me take the paines to hang you:
It is but halfe an howers exercise.
Seg. You are still in your knauery:
But sith I cannot haue his life,
I will procure his banishment for euer: Come on sirra.
Clo. Yes forsooth, I come: laugh at him I pray you. *Exeunt.*

Enter Mucedorus solus.

Mu. From Amadine and from her Fathers Court,
With Gould and Siluer, and with rich rewards,
Flowing from the bankes of Golden treasures:

More

The Comedie

More may I boast and say, but I
Was neuer Shepheard in such dignitie.

Enter the Messenger and the Clowne.

Mes. All haile, worthy Shepheard.
Clo. All raine, lowsie Shepheard.
Mu. Welcome my friendes: from whence come you?
Mes. The King and *Amadine* greete thee well,
And after greeting done, bids thee depart the Court:
Shepheard be gone.
Clo. Shepheard take law-legs, flie away Shepheard.
Mu. Whose wordes are these, came these from *Amadine?*
Mes. Aie from *Amadine*. *Clo.* Aie from *Amadine.*
Mu. Ah luckless fortune, worse then *Phaetons* tale,
My former blisse, is now become my bale.
Clo. What, wilt thou poyson thy selfe?
Mu. My former Heauen, is now become my Hell.
Clo. The worst Ale-house that euer I came in, in all my life.
Mu. What shall I doe?
Clo. Euen goe hange thy selfe halfe an houre.
Mu. Can *Amadine* so churlishly commaund
To banish the Shepheard from her fathers Court?
Mes. What should Shepheards doe in the Court?
Clo. What should Shepheards doe amongst vs?
Haue we not Lords enough on vs in the Court?
Mu. Why Shepheards are men, and Kings are no more.
Mes. Shepheards are men, and maisters ouer their flocke.
Clo. That's a lie, who payes them their wages then?
Mes. Well, you are alwayes interrupting of me:
But you were best to looke to him, least you hang for him,
When he is gone. *Exit.*

The Clowne singes.

Clo. And you shall hang for companie,
For leauing me alone:
Shepheard stand foorth, and heare my sentence.
Shepheard be gone within three dayes, in paine of my displeasure: Shepheard be gone, Shepheard begon, begon, begon, begon Shepheard, Shepheard Shepheard. *Exit.*

Mu. And must I goe? and must I needes depart?

Ye

of Mucedorus.

Ye goodly groues,partakers of my songs,
In time tofore when Fortune did not frowne,
Powre foorth your plaints,and waile a while with me:
And thou bright Sunne my comfort in the cold,
Hide,hide thy face,and leaue me comfortlesse.
Yee holsome hearbes,and sweete smelling sauours,
Yea each thing else prolonging life of man.
Change,change your wonted course,
That I wanting your ayde, in wofull sort may die.

Enter Amadine, and Ariena her maid.

Am. *Ariena*, if any body aske for mee,
Make some excuse, till I returne,
Ari. What and *Segasto* call? *Exit.*
An. Do thou the like to him, I meane not to stay long.
Mu. This voyce so sweete my pining spirits reuiues.
Am. Shepheard well met, tell me how thou doest.
Mu, I linger life, yet wish for speedy death.
Am. Shepheard although thy banishment already
Be decreed,and all against my will,yet *Amadine.*
Mu. Ah *Amadine*, to heare of banishment, is death;
I,double death to me: but since I must depart,one thing I craue.
Am. Say on with all my heart.
Mu. That in absence, either farre or neere,
You honour me as Seruant with your name.
Am. Not so.   Mu. And why?
Am. I honour thee as Soueraigne of my heart.
Mu. A Shepheard and a Soueraigne,nothing like.
Am Yet like enough,where there is no dislike.
Mu. Yet great dislike,or else no banishment.
Am. Shepheard, it is only *Segasto* that procures thy banish-
Mu, Vnworthy wights are more in iealosie.   (ment
Am. Would God they would free thee from banishment,or
likewise banish me.
Mu. Amen say I, to haue your company.
Am. Well Shepheard sith thou suffrest this for my sake,
With thee in exile also let me liue.
On this condition Shepheard,thou canst loue.
Mu. No longer loue,no longer let me liue.

Am.

The Comedie

Am. Of late I loued one indeed; now loue I none but onely
Mu. Thanks worthy Princesse: I burne likewise, (thee,
Yet smother vp the blast:
I dare not promise what I may performe.
  Am. Well Shepheard, harke what I shall say,
I will returne vnto my Fathers Court,
There for to prouide me of such necessaries
As for my iourney I shall thinke most fit:
This being done, I will returne to thee,
Do thou therefore appoint the place
Where wee may meete.
  Mu. Downe in the valley, where I slue the Beare,
And there doth grow a faire broad branched Beech,
That ouershades a Well: So who comes first,
Let them abide the happie meeting of vs both:
How like you this?   *Am.* I like it very well.
  Mu. Now if you please you may appoint the time.
  Am. Full three howers hence, God willing, I will returne.
  Mu. The thankes that *Paris* gaue the Grecian Queene,
the like doth *Mucedorus* yeeld.
  Am. Then *Mucedorus* for three howers farewell.   *Exit.*
  Mu. Your departure Lady breeds a priuie paine.   *Exit.*
        Enter Segasto solus.
  Seg. Tis well *Segasto*, that thou hast thy will,
Should such a Shepheard, such a simple Swaine as he,
Eclipse thy credite famous through the Court?
No, plie *Segasto* plie, let it not in *Aragon* be sayd,
A Shepheard hath *Segstoes* honour wonne.
        Enter Mouse the Clowne, calling his Maister.
  Clo. What, hoe Maister, will you come away?
  Seg. Will you come hither I pray you: whats the matter?
  Clo. Why is it not past eleuen a clocke?   *Seg.* How then sir?
  Clo. I pray you come away to dinner.
  Seg. I pray you come hither.
  Clo. Heer's such adoe with you, will you neuer come?
  Seg. I pray you sir, what newes of the message I sent you a-
bout.
  Clo. I tell you all the Messes be on the Table already,
                                                    There

of Mucedorus.

There wants not so much as a messe of Mustard, halfe an houre
 Seg. Come sir, your minde is all vpon your belly, (agoe.
You haue forgotten what I bid you doe.
 Clo. Faith I know nothing, but you bad me go to breakfast.
 Seg. Was that all?
 Clo. Faith I haue forgotten it; the very scent of the Meate made me, hath forgot it quite.
 Seg. You haue forgotten the arrand I bid you doe.
 Clo. What arrant? an arrant Knaue, or an arrant Whore?
 Seg. Why thou Knaue, did I not bid thee banish the Shep-
 Clo. O the Shepheards bastard. (heard?
 Seg. I tell thee, the Shepheards banishment.
 Clo. I tell you the Shepheards Bastard shall be well kept; Ile looke to it my selfe: but I pray you, come away to dinner.
 Seg. Then you will not tell me whether you haue banished him or no?
 Clo. Why I cannot say, Banishment, and you would giue me a thousand pounds to say so.
 Seg. Why you hourson slaue, haue you forgotten that I sent you, and another, to driue away the Shepheard?
 Clo. What an Asse are you: heer's a stirre in deed; Heer's message, arrant, banishment and I cannot tell what?
 Seg. I pray you sir, shall I know whether you haue droue him away?
 Clo. Faith I thinke I haue: and you will not beleeue me, aske my Staffe.
 Seg. Why, can thy Staffe tell?
 Clo. Why, he was with me too.
 Seg. Then happie I, that haue obtaind my will.
 Clo. And happier I, if you would goe to dinner.
 Seg. Come sirra, follow me.
 Clo. I warrant you I will not loose an inch of you, now you are going to dinner: I promise you, I thought seauen yeare before I could get him away. *Exeunt.*

Enter Amadine solus.

 Am. God graunt my long delay procures no harme,
Nor this my tarrying frustrate my pretence:
My Mucedorus surely stayes for mee,
                        D.   And

The Comedie

And thinkes me ouer-long, at length I come,
My present promise to performe:
Ah what a thing is firme vnfaigned loue,
What is it which true loue dares not attempt?
My Father he may make, but I must match:
Segasto loues, but *Amadine* must like
Where likes her best; compulsion is a thrall:
No, no, the heartie choyce, is all in all.
The Shepheards vertue *Amadine* esteemes.
But what? me thinkes my Shepheard is not come:
I muse at that, the hower is at hand:
Well, here Ile rest till *Mucedorus* come.   *She sits downe.*

Enter Bremo looking about, hastily takes hold of her.

Bre. A happy prey; now *Bremo* feed on flesh:
Dainties *Bremo* dainties, thy hungry panch to fill,
Now glut thy greedy guts with luke-warme bloud:
Come fight with me, I long to see thee dead.
  Am. How can she fight that weapons cannot weeld?
  Bre. What, canst not fight? then lie thee downe and die.
  Am. What, must I die?
  Bre. What neede these words, I thirst to sucke thy bloude?
  Am. Yet pittie me, and let me liue a while.
  Bre. No pittie I, Ile feede vpon thy flesh,
Ile teare thy body peece-meale ioynt from ioynt.
  Am. Ah how I want my Shepheards company.
  Bre. Ile crush thy bones betwixt two Oken trees.
  Am. Haste Shepheard haste, or els thou com'st too late.
  Bre. Ile sucke the sweetnes from thy Marrow-bones.
  Am. Ah spare, ah spare to shed my guiltlesse bloud.
  Bre. With this my Bat, will I beate out thy braines;
Downe downe I say, prostrat thy selfe vpon the ground.
  Am. Then *Mucedorus*, farewell; my hoped ioyes, farewell:
Yea, farewell life, and welcome present death,   *She kneeles.*
To thee, O God, I yeeld my dying Ghost:
  Bre. Now *Bremo*, play thy part.
How now, What sudden chaunce is this?
My Limmes doe tremble, and my Sinowes shake:

My

of Mucedorus.

My vnweakned Armes hath lost their former force:
Ah *Bremo, Bremo*, what a foyle hast thou,
That yet at no time wast afraid,
To dare the greatest Gods to fight with thee,   *He strikes.*
And now wants strength for one downe driuing blow?
Ah how my courage fayles, when I should strike;
Some now-come spirit abiding in my breast;
Shall I spare her *Bremo*? Spare her, do not kill,
Saith spare her, which neuer spared any.
To it *Bremo*, to it: say againe;
I cannot weeld my weapons in my hand:
Me thinkes I should not strike so faire a one,
I thinke her Beautie hath bewitcht my force,
Or else within me, altered Natures course.
Aie Woman! wilt thou liue in Woods with me?
    Am. Faine would I line, yet loth to liue in Woods.
    Bre. Thou shalt not choose, it shall be as I say,
And therefore follow me.   *Exeunt.*

    Enter Mucedorus solus.

    Muc. It was my will an houre agoe and more,
As was my promise, for to make returne;
But other businesse hindred my pretence.
It is a world to see, when man appoyntes,
And purposely one certaine thing decrees,
How many thinges may hinder his intent:
What one would wish, the same is fartheft off,
But yet th'appoynted time can not be past;
Nor hath her presence yet preuented me:
Well, heere Ile stay, and expect her comming.
    They cry within, Hold him, hold him.
    Mu. Some one or other is pursued, no doubt,
Perhaps some search for me; tis good to doubt the worst,
Therefore Ile be gone.   *Exit.*

    Cry within, Hold him, hold him: Enter Mouse
    the Clowne with a Pot.
    Cl. Hold him, hold him, hold him: heer's a stirre indeed: here came hew after the crier; & I was set close at mother *Nips* house,

D 2   and

The Comedie

and there I cald for three pots of ale, as tis the maner of vs Courtiers. now sirra. I had taken the maiden-head of two of them: Now as I was lifting vp the third to my mouth, there came, hold him, hold him: now I could not tell whom to catch hold on; but I am sure I caught one, perchance a may be in this pot: well Ile see: Masse I cannot see him yet: Well, Ile looke a little further: Masse he is a little slaue if a be here: why heer's no body: all this goes well yet. But if the old Trot should come for her pot, I marie there's the matter. But I care not, Ile face her out, and cal her old rustie, dustie, mustie, tustie, crustie Fierbrand and worse then all that, and so face her out of her pot, but soft, heere she comes.

Enter the old Woman

Old W. Come you knaue, where's my pot you knaue?

Clo. Goe looke your pot, come not to me for your pot, twere good for you.

Old. Thou liest thou knaue, thou hast my pot.

Clo. You lie and you say it: I your pot? I know what Ile say. Why, what wilt thou say?

Clo. But say I haue him, and thou dar'st.

Old. Why thou knaue, thou hast not onely my pot, but my drinke vnpayd for.

Clo. You lie like an old: I will not say whore.

Old. Doest thou call me whore? Ile cap thee for my pot.

Clo. Cap me and thou darest:
Search me whether I haue it or no.

She searcheth him, and he drinketh ouer her head, and casteth downe the Pot, she stumbleth at it: then they tall together by the eares: she takes vp her Pot, and goes out.

Enter Seg st.

Seg. How now sirra, what's the matter?

Clo. Oh Flies Master, Flies.

Seg. Flies, where are they?

Clo. Oh, heere Maister all about your face.

Seg. Why thou liest I thinke thou art mad.

Clo. Why Maister, I haue killed a dung-cart full at the least.

Seg. Go too sirra, leauing this idle talke, giue eare to me.

Clo. How, giue you one of my eares?

Not

of Mucedorus.

Not and you were ten Maisters.

Seg. Why sir, I bid you giue eare to my words.

Clo. I tell you, I will not be made a Curtall for no mans plea-(sure.

Seg. I tell thee, attend what I say:
Goe thy wayes straight and reare the whole Towne.

Clo. How, reare the whole Towne? euen goe your selfe, it is more then I can doe: Why do you thinke I can reare a Towne, that can scarce reare a Pot of Ale to my head: I should reare a Towne, should I not?

Seg. Goe to the Constable, and make a Priuie search, For the Shepheard is runne away with the Kings Daughter.

Clo. How, is the Shepheard run away with the kings daughter, or is the Kings daughter run away with the Shepheard?

Seg. I cannot tell; but they are both gone togeather.

Clo. What a foole is she, to runne away with the Shepheard? Why, I thinke I am a litle handsomer Man, then the Shepheard, my selfe. But tell me Maister; must I make a Priuie search, or search in the Priuie?

Seg. Why, doest thou thinke they will be there?

Clo. I cannot tell.

Seg. Well then, search euery where, Leaue no place vnsearcht for them. *Exit.*

Clo. Oh, now am I in an Office: now will I to that old firebrands house, and will not leaue one place vnsearched: Nay Ile to the Ale-stand, and drinke as long as I can stand: and when I haue done, Ile let out all the rest, to see if he be not hid in the Barrell: and if I find him not there, Ile to the Cupbord; Ile not leaue one corner of her house vnsearched: y'fayth ye old crust, I will be with you now. *Exit.*

Sound Musicke.

Enter the King of Valentia, Anselmo, Roderigo, Lord Borachius, with others.

King V t. Enough of Musicke, it but ads to torment; Delights to vexed spirits, are as Dates Set to a sickly man; which rather cloy, then comfort: Let mee intreate you, to intreat no more.

Rod. Let your strings sleepe; haue done there. *Let the musicke*

Kin. V. Mirth to a soule disturb'd, are embers turn'd, (*cease*

Which

The Comedie

Which sudden gleame, with molestation,
But sooner loose their sight-fort;
Tis Gold bestowd vpon a Ryotor,
Which not relieues, but murders him:
Tis a Drugge giuen to the healthfull,
Which infects, not cures.
How can a Father that hath lost his Sonne,
A Prince both wise, vertuous, and valiant,
Take pleasure in the idle actes of Time?
No, no; till *Mucedorus* I shall see againe,
All ioy is comfortlesse, all pleasure paine.

   Ans. Your Sonne (my Lord) is well.
   K.V. I pre-thee, speake that thrise.
   Anl. The Prince your Sonne, is safe.
   K.V. Oh where *Anselmo?* surfet me with that.
   Anl. In *Aragon* my Liege; and at his parture,
Bound my secrecie
By his affectious loue, not to disclose it:
But care of him, and pittie of your age,
Makes my tongue blab, what my breast vow'd concealment.

   K.V. Thou not deceiu'st me; I euer thought thee
What I find thee now, an vpright loyall man.
But what desire, or young-fed humour
Nurst within the braine,
Drew him so priuatly to *Aragon?*

   Ans. A forcing Adamant,
Loue, mixt with feare and doubtfull ielousie,
Whether report guilded a worthlesse truncke,
Or *Amadine* deserued her high extolment.

   K.V. See our prouision be in readinesse,
Collect vs followers, of the comliest hue,
For our chiefe guardions, we will thither wend:
The christall eye of Heauen shall not thrise wincke,
Nor the greene Flood, sixe times his shoulders turne,
Till we salute the *Aragonian* King.
Ails sicke speake loudly, now the season's apt,
For former dolours are in pleasure wrapt.   *Exeunt omnes.*

                                     Enter

of Mucedorus.

Enter Mucedorus to disguise himselfe.

Mu. Now *Mucedorus*, whither wilt thou goe?
Home to thy Father, to thy natiue soyle,
Or trie some long abode within these Woodes:
Well I will hence depart and hie me home.
What, hie me home said I? that may not be,
In *Amadine* restes my felicitie.
Then *Mucedorus*, doe as thou didst decree,
Attire thee Hermit-like within these Groues,
Walke often to the Beech, and view the Well,
Make Settles there, and seat thy selfe thereon,
And when thou feelest thy selfe to be athirst,
Then drinke a heartie draught to *Amadine*,
No doubt she thinkes on thee,
And will one day come pledge thee, at this Well.
Come Habite, thou art fit for me,   *He disguiseth himselfe.*
No Shepheard now, a Hermite must I be:
Mee thinkes this fittes me very well,
Now must I learne to beare a walking Staffe,
And exercise some grauitie withall.

Enter the Clowne.

Clo. Heer's through the woods, and through the woods,
To looke out a Shepheard, and a stray Kings Daughter:
But soft, who haue we heere? what art thou?

Mu. I am an Hermite.

Clo. An Emmet, I neuer saw such a bigge Emmet in all my
life before.

Mu. I tell you sir, I am an Hermite, one that leades a solitary
life within these Woods.

Clo. O, I know thee now; thou art her that eates vp all the
Hips and Hawes: wee could not haue one peece of fatte Bacon
for thee a l this yeare.

Mu. Thou doest mistake me: But I pray thee tell me, who
doest thou seeke in these Woods?

Clo. What doe I seeke? for a stray Kinges Daughter,
Runne away with a Shepheard.

Mu. A stray Kinges Daughter, run away with a Shepheard,
Wherefore, canst thou tell?

                                                       Clo.

The Comedie

Clo. Yes that I can, tis this; my Maister & *Amadine*, walking one day abroad, neerer to these Woodes then they were vsed (about what I cannot tell) but towards them comes runing a great Beare: now my Maister he plaide the man, and ran away; and *Amadine*, crying after him: now sir, comes mee a Shepheard and hee strikes off the Beares Head: now whether the Beare were dead before or no, I cannot tell; for bring twentie Beares before me, and bind their hands and feete, and Ile kill them all. Now euer since *Amadine* hath bin in loue with the Shepheard, and for good-will shee's euen run away with the Shepheard.

Mu. What maner of man was he, canst describe him vnto me?

Clo. Scribe him, aye I warrant you that I can; a was a little, low, broad, tall, narrow bigge, wel-fauoured fellow: a Ierkin of white cloth, and buttons of the same cloth.

Mu. Thou describest him well: but if I chaunce to see any such, pray you where shall I find you, or what's your name?

Clo. My name is called, Maister *Mouse*.

Mu. Oh Maister *Mouse*, I pray you what Office might you beare in the Court?

Clo. Mary sir I am a Rusher of the Stable.

Mu. Oh, Vsher of the Table.

Clo. Nay I say Rusher, and I prooue mine Office good: for looke sir, when any comes from vnder the Sea, or so, & a Dogge chaunce to blow his nose backward, then with a whippe I giue him the good time of the day & strow Rushes presently; therefore I am a Rusher: a high Office I promise yee.

Mu. But where shall I find you in the Court?

Clo. Why where it is best beeing, either in the Kitchin a eating, or in the Butterie drinking: but if you come, I will prouide for thee a peece of Beefe & Brewes knuckle deepe in fatte: pray you take paines; remember maister *Mouse*.   *Exit.*

Mu. Ay sir, I warrant, I will not forget you.
Ah *Amadine*! What should become of thee?
Whither shouldst thou goe so long vnknowne?
With Watch and Ward each passage is beset,
So that she cannot long escape vnknowne.
Doubtlesse she hath lost her selfe within these Woods,
And wandring too and fro, she seekes the Well,

Which

of Mucedorus.

Which yet she can not find; therfore will I seeke her out. *Exit.*

Enter Bremo and Amadine.

Bre. Amadine, how like you *Bremo*, and his Woods?

Ama. As like the Woods, of *Bremoes* crueltie:
Though I were dumbe, and could not answere him,
The Beastes themselues would with relenting teares,
Bewaile thy sauage and vnhumaine deedes.

Bre. My Loue, why dost thou murmure to thy selfe?
Speake louder, for thy *Bremo* heares thee not.

Am. My *Bremo*, no, the Shepheard is my Loue.

Bre. Haue I not saued thee from sudden death,
Giuing thee leaue to liue, that thou mightst loue,
And dost thou whet me on to crueltie?
Come kisse me (sweete) for all my fauours past.

Am. I may not *Bremo*, and therefore pardon me.

Bre. See how she flinges away from me,
I will follow, and giue attend to her.
Denie my Loue, a worme of Beautie:
I will chastice thee: come, come,
Prepare thy head vpon the Blocke.

Am. O spare me *Bremo*, Loue should limit life,
Not to be made a murderer of himselfe.
If thou wilt glut thy louing heart with blood,
Encounter with the Lion, or the Beare,
And like a Woolfe, prey not vpon a Lambe.

Bre. Why then dost thou repine at me?
If thou wilt loue me, thou shalt be my Queene,
I will crowne thee with a Complet made of Iuorie,
And make the Rose and Lillie waite on thee:
Ile rend the burly Branches from the Oxe,
To shadow thee from burning Sunne.
The Trees shall spread themselues where thou dost goe,
And as they spread, Ile trace along with thee.

Am. You may; for who but you

Bre. Thou shalt be fedde with Quailes and Partriges,
With Black-birds, Larkes, Thrushes, and Nightingales:
Thy drinke shall be Goates milke and cristall Water,
Distilled from the fountaines, and the clearest Springes:

E.   And

The Comedie

And all the dainties that the Woods afford,
Ile freely giue thee, to obtaine thy loue.
   Am. You may, for who but you.
   Bre. The day Ile spend, to recreate my Loue
With all the pleasures that I can deuise:
And in the night, Ile be thy bedfellow,
And louingly imbrace thee in mine armes.
   Am. One may, so may not you.
   Bre. The Satyrs & the Wood-nimphes shall attend on thee,
And lull thee asleepe with Musicks sound:
And in the morning when thou doest awake,
The Larke shall sing, good-morrow to my Queene:
And whilest he singes, Ile kisse mine *Amadine*.
   Am. You may, for who but you.
   Bre. When thou art vp, the Wood-lanes shall be strowed
With Violets, Cowslips, and sweete Marigolds,
For thee to trample and to trace vpon:
And I will teach thee how to kill the Deare,
To chase the Hart, and how to rouse the Roe,
If thou wilt liue to loue and honour me.
   Am. You may, for who but you.
      Enter Mucedorus.
   Bre. Welcome sir, an houre agoe I lookt for such a guest:
Be merrie Wench, weele haue a frolicke Feast;
Heer's flesh enough for to suffice vs both:
Say sirra, wilt thou fight, or doest thou meane to die?
   Mu. I want a Weapon, how can I fight?
   Bre. Thou wants a Weapon, why then thou yeeldst to die.
   Mu. I say not so; I doe not yeeld to die.
   Bre. Thou shalt not chuse, I long to see thee dead.
   Am. Yet spare him *Bremo*, spare him.
   Bre. Away I say, I will not spare him.
   Mu. Yet giue me leaue to speake.
   Bre. Thou shalt not speake.
   Am. Yet giue him leaue to speake, for my sake.
   Bre. Speake on; but be not ouer-long.
   Mu. In time of yore, when men like brutish Beastes,
Did lead their liues in loathsome Celles and Woods,

                                  And

of Mucedorus.

And wholly gaue themselues to witlesse Will;
A rude vnruly route: then, man to man became,
A present prey, then Might preuailed,
The weakest went to Walles:
Right was vnknowne, for Wrong was all in all:
As men thus liued in their great out-rage,
Behold one *Orpheus* came, as Poets tell,
And them from Rudenesse vnto Reason brought:
Who lead by Reason, some forsooke the Woods,
In stead of Caues, they built them Castles strong;
Cities and Townes were founded by them then:
Glad were they, they found such ease,
And in the end, they grew to perfect amitie,
Waying their former wickednesse:
They tearm'd the time wherein they liued then,
A Golden age, a goodly Golden age.
Now *Bremo*, (for so I heare thee called)
If men which liued tofore, as thou doest now,
Wilde in Wood, addicted all to spoyle,
Returned were by worthy *Orpheus* meanes;
Let me like *Orpheus*, cause thee to returne
From Murther, Bloodshed, and like crueltie:
What should we fight before we haue a cause?
No, lets liue, and loue togeather faythfully.
Ile fight for thee.

Bre. Fight for me, or die: or fight, or else thou diest.
Am. Hold *Bremo*, hold.
Bre. Away I say, thou troublest me.
Am. You promised me to make me your Queene.
Bre. I did, I meane no lesse.
Am. You promised that I should haue my will.
Bre. I did, I meane no lesse.
Am. Then saue this Hermites life, for he may saue vs both.
Bre. At thy request Ile spare him; but neuer any, after him.
Say Hermite, what canst thou doe?
Mu. Ile waite on thee, sometime vpon thy Queene:
Such seruice shalt thou shortly haue, as *Bremo* neuer had.
Exeunt.

The Comedie

Enter Segasto, the Clowne, and Rumbelo.

Seg. Come sirs, what shall I neuer haue you finde out *Amadine* and the Shepheard?

Clo. And I haue bene through the Woods, and through the Woods, and could see nothing but an Emmet.

Ru. why I see a thousand Emmets: thou meanst a little one.

Clo. Nay, that Emmet that I saw, was bigger then thou art.

Ru. Bigger then I, what a foole haue you to your man? I pray you Maister turne him away.

Seg. But dost thou heare, was he not a man?

Clo. Thinke he was, for he sayd he did lead a Saltsellers life about the woods.

Seg. Thou wouldest say, a solitarie life about the woods.

Clo. I thinke it was so in deed.

Ru. I thought what a foole thou art.

Clo. Thou art a wise man: Why he did nothing but sleepe since he went.

Seg. But tell me *Mouse*, How did he goe?

Clo. In a white Gowne, and a white Hat on his head, And a staffe in his hand.

Seg. I thought so, it was an Hermite that walked a solitarie life in the woods. Well, get you to dinner; and after, neuer leaue seeking, till you bring some newes of them, or Ile hang you both. *Exit.*

Clo. How now *Rumbelo*, what shall we do now?

Ru. Faith Ile home to dinner, and afterward to sleepe.

Clo. Why then thou wilt be hanged.

Ru. Faith I care not, for I know I shall neuer finde them: Well, Ile once more abroad; and If I cannot find them, Ile neuer come home againe.

Clo. I tell thee what *Rumbelo*, thou shalt goe in at one ende of the wood, and I at the other, and we will meete both together in the midst.

Ru. Content, let's away to dinner. *Exeunt*

Enter Mucedorus solus.

Mu. Vnknowne to any heere within these Woods, With bloudy *Bremo* do I leade my life: The Monster he, doth murder all he meetes,

He

of Mucedorus.

He spareth none, and none doth him escape:
Who would continue, who but onely I
In such a cruell cutthroats companie?
Yet *Amadine* is there, how can I chuse;
A silly soule, how often times she sits
And sighes, and cals, come Shepheard come:
Sweete *Mucedorus* come and set me free,
When *Mucedorus* (Peasant) stands her by,
But heere she comes: What newes faire Lady,
As you walke these woods? *Enter Amadine.*

Am. Ah Hermite, none but bad,
And such as thou knowest.

Mu. How do you like your *Bremo*, and his woods?

Am. Not my *Bremo*, nor his *Bremo* woods.

Mu. And why not yours? me thinkes he loues you well.

Am. I like not him; his loue to me is nothing worth.

Mu. Lady, in this, me thinkes you offer wrong,
To hate the man, that euer loues you best.

Am. Ah Hermite, I take no pleasure in his loue:
Neither doth *Bremo* like me best.

Mu. Pardon my boldnesse, faire Lady; sith we both
May safely talke now, out of *Bremoes* sight:
Vnfold to me, so if you please, the full discourse
How, when, and why, you came into these Woods,
And fell into this bloody Butchers hands.

Am. Hermite I will: Of late a worthy Shepheard I did loue.

Mu. A Shepheard (Lady) sure a man vnfit to match with you?

Am. Hermite, this is true: and when we had.

Mu. Stay there, the Wild-man comes,
Referre the rest vntill another time.

Enter Bremo.

Bre. What secret tale is this? What whispring haue we heere?
Villaine, I charge thee tell thy tale againe.

Mu. If needes I must, loe heere it is againe.
When as we both had lost the sight of thee,
It grieu'd vs both; but specially thy Queene:
Who in thy absence, euer feares the worst,
Least some mischaunce befall your royall Grace.

The Comedie

Shall my sweete *Bremo* wander through the Woods,
Toyle too and fro, for to redresse my want,
Hazard his life, and all to chearish me?
I like not this, quoth she:
And thereupon crau'd to know of me
If I could teach her handle Weapons well.
My answere was, I had small skill therein,
But gladsome (mighty King) to learne of thee:
And this was all.

Bre. Wast so, none can dislike of this;
Ile teach you both to fight: but first, my Queene begin,
Heere, take this Weapon, see how thou canst vse it.

Am. This is too bigge, I can not weeld it in my arme.

Bre. Ist so? weele haue a knottie Crab-tree staffe for thee:
But sirra, tell me, what sayest thou?

Mu. With all my heart, I willing am to learne.

Bre. Then take my Staffe, and see how thou canst weeld it.

Mu. First teach me how to hold it in my hand.

Bre. Thou hold'st it well: looke how he doth,
Thou mayest the sooner learne.

Mu. Next tell me how, and when tis best to strike.

Bre. Tis best to strike, when time doth serue;
Tis best to loose no time.

Mu. Then now or neuer, is my time to strike.

Bre. And when thou strikest, be sure to hit the Head.

Mu. The Head?

Bre. The very Head.

Mu. Then haue at thine: *He strikes him downe dead.*
So, lie there and die; a death no doubt, according to desert,
Or else a worse, as thou deseru'st a worse.

Am. It glads my heart, this Tyrants death to see.

Mu. Now Lady, it remaines in you,
To end the Tale you lately had begun,
Being interrupted by this wicked wight:
You sayd, you loued a Shepheard.

Am. I so I doe, and none but onely him;
And will doe still, as long as life shall last.

Mu. But tell me Lady, sith I set you free,

What

of Mucedorus.

What courfe of life doe you intend to take?
 Am. I will difguifed wander through the world,
Till I haue found him out.
 Mu. How if you find your Shepheard in thefe Woods?
 Am. Ah! none fo happy then as *Amadine.*
He difguifeth himfelfe.
 Mu. In tract of time, a man may alter much:
Say Lady, Doe you know your Shepheard well?
 Am. My *Mucedorus*: hath he fet me free?
 Mu. He hath fet thee free.
 Am. And liued fo long vnknowne to *Amadine.*
 Mu Ay that's a queftion whereof you may not be refolued,
You khow that I am bannifht from the Court?
I know likewife each paffage is befet,
So that we cannot long efcape vnknowne:
Therefore my will is this that we returne:
Right through the thickets to the Wild-mans Caue,
And there a while liue on his prouifion,
Vntill the fearch and narrow Watch be paft:
This is my counfell, and I thinke it beft.
 Am. I thinke the very fame.
 Muc. Come, let's be gone.

*The Clowne fearcheth, and falles ouer the wild-man,
and fo carries him away.*

 Clo. Nay foft fir; are you heere? a bots on you,
I was like to be hanged for not finding you:
We would borrow a certaine ftray Kings daughter of you:
A Wench, a Wench fir, we would haue.
 Muc. A Wench of mee? Ile make thee eate my fword.
 Clo. Oh Lord; nay & you are fo lufty, Iln call a cooling card
for you: Ho Maifter, Maifter, I, come away quickly. *Enter Seg.*
 Seg. What's the matter?
 Clo. Looke Maifter: *Amadine* & the Shepheard; ô braue.
 Seg. What Minion, haue I found you out?
 Clo Nay that's a lie, I found her out my felfe.
 Seg. Thou gadding hufwife, What caufe hadft thou
to gadde abroad,

When

The Comedie

When as thou knowest our Wedding day so niee
  Am. Not so *Segasto*, no such thing in hand:
Shew your Assurance, then Ile answere you.
  Seg. Thy Fathers Promise, my assurance is.
  Am. But what he promist, he hath not performde.
  Seg. It restes in thee for to performe the same.
  Am. Not I.
  Seg. And why?
  Am. So is my will; and therefore euen so.
  Clo. Maister, with a none, none, no.
  Seg. Ah wicked villaine, art thou heere?
  Mu. What needes these wordes? we waigh them not.
  Seg. We waigh them not, proud Shepheard, I scorne thy com-
  Clo. Weele not haue a corner of thy companie. (panie.
  Mu. I scorne not thee, nor yet the least of thine.
  Clo. That's a lie; a would haue kild me with his pugs-nando.
  Seg. This stoutnesse *Amadine*, contentes me not.
  Am. Then seeke another, that may you better please.
  Mu. Well *Amadine*, it onely restes in thee,
(Without delay) to make thy choyce of three:
There standes *Segasto*, heere a Shepheard standes,
There standes the third: now make thy choyce.
  Clo. A Lord (at the least) I am.
  Am. My choyce is made; for I will none but thee.
  Seg. A worthy Mate (no doubt) for such a Wife.
  Mu. And *Amadine*, why, wilt thou none but mee?
I can not keepe thee as thy Father did;
I haue no Landes for to maintaine thy state:
Moreouer, if thou meane to be my Wife,
Commonly this must be thy vse,
To bed at midnight, vp at foure;
Drudge all day, and trudge from place to place,
Whereby our dayly victuall for to winne:
And last of all, which is the worst of all;
No Princesse then, but plaine a Shepheards wife.
  Clo. Then God gee-you good morrow gooddy Shepheard.
  Am. It shall not need; if *Amadine* doe liue,
Thou shalt be crowned King of Aragon.

                                            Clo.

of Mucedorus.

Clo. Oh Maister laugh: when hee's King, the I'le be a Queene.
Mu. Then know that, which neretofore was knowne;
I am no Shepheard, no Aragonian I,
But borne of Royall blood: my Father's of Valencia King,
My Mother Queene: who for thy sacred sake,
Tooke this hard taske in hand.
Am. Ah how I ioy, my fortune is so good.
Seg. Well now I see Segasto shall not speed:
But Mucedorus, I as much doe ioy
To see thee heere within our Court of Aragon,
As if a Kingdome had befalne me this time:
I with my heart, surrender her to thee;

He giues her to him.

And looke what right to Amadine I haue.
Clo. What Barnes doore, and borne where my Father was Constable; a bots on thee: how dost thee?
Mu. Thankes Segasto: but yet you leueld at the Crowne.
Clo. Maister, beare this, and beare all.
Seg. Why so sir?
Clo. He sees you take a Goose by the crowne.
Seg. Goe to sir, away, post you to the King,
Whose heart is fraught with carefull doubts,
Glad him vp, and tell him these good newes,
And we will follow as fast as we may.
Clo. I goe Maister, I runne Maister.   *Exeunt.*

Enter the King and Collin.

King. Breake heart, and end my pallade woes,
My Amadine, the comfort of my life:
How can I ioy, except she were in sight?
Her absence breedes sorrow to my soule,
And with a thunder, breakes my heart in twaine.
Col. Forbeare those passions, gentle King,
And you shall see t'will turne vnto the best,
And bring your soule to quiet and to ioy.
King. Such ioy as death, I doe assure me that,
And nought but death, vnlesse of her I heare,
And that with speed, I cannot sigh thus long:
But what a tumult doe I heare within?

F.   They

The Comedie

A vey cry within, Ioy and Happinesse.

Col. I heare a noyse of ouer-passing ioy
Within the Court: my Lord, be of good comfort:
And heere comes one in haste.

Enter the Clowne running.

Clo. A King, a King, a King.
Col. Why how now sirra, what's the matter?
Clo. O tis newes for a King, tis worth money.
Kin. Why sirra, thou shalt haue siluer and gold, if it be good.
Clo. O tis good, tis good: *Amadine.*
Kin. O what of her? tell me, and I will make thee a Knight.
Clo. How, a Spright? no by Lady, I will not be a Spright:
Maisters get you away, if I be a spright, I shall be so leane,
I shall make you all afrayde.
Col. Thou sot, the King meanes to make thee a Gentleman.
Clo. Why, I shall want Parrell.
Kin. Thou shalt want for nothing.
Clo. Then stand away, strike vp thy selfe: heere they come.

Enter Segasto, Mucedorus, and Amadine.

Am. My gracious Father, pardon thy disloyall Daughter.
Kin. What, doe mine eyes behold my Daughter *Amadine?*
Rise vp deare Daughter, and let these my imbracing Armes
Shew some token of thy Fathers ioy,
Which euer since thy departure, hath languished in sorrow.
Am. Deare Father, neuer were your sorrowes
Greater then my griefes:
Neuer you so desolate, as I comfortlesse:
Yet neuerthelesse, acknowledging my selfe
To be the cause of both; on bended knees,
I humbly craue your Pardon.
Kin. Ile pardon thee deare Daughter: but as for him.
Am. Ay Father, what of him?
Kin. As sure as I am King and weare the Crowne,
I will revenge on that accursed wretch.
Mu. Yet worthy Prince, worke not thy will in wrath, shew
Kin. I, such fauour as thou deseruest. (fauour.
Mu. I doe deserue the Daughter of a King.
Kin. Oh impudent; a Shepheard, and so insolent?

Mu.

of Mucedorus.

Mu. No Shepheard I, but a worthy Prince.
Kin. In faire conceit, not Princely borne.
Mu. Yes Princely borne; my Father is a King,
My Mother a Queene, and of *Valencia* both.
 Kin. What *Mucedorus*? Welcome to our Court:
What cause hadst thou to come to me disguisde?
 Mu. No cause to feare, I caused no offence,
But this; desiring thy Daughters vertues for to see,
Disguisde my selfe from out my fathers Court,
Vnknowne to any, in secret I did rest,
And passed many troubles neere to death:
So hath your Daughter my partaker been,
As you shall know hereafter more at large:
Desiring you, you will giue her to mee,
Euen as mine owne, and soueraigne of my life:
Then shall I thinke my trauels are well spent.
 Kin. With all my heart : but this,
Segasto claymes my Promise made tofore,
That he should haue her as his onely wife,
Before my Counsell, when we came from Warre.
Segasto, may I craue thee let it passe,
And giue *Amadine* as wife to *Mucedorus*?
 Seg. With all my heart, were it a farre greater thing;
And what I may to furnish vp their rites,
With pleasing sportes and pastimes, you shall see.
 Kin. Thankes good *Segasto*, I will thinke of this.
 Mu. Thankes good my Lord; and while I liue,
Account of mee in what I can, or may.
 Am. And good *Segasto*, these great courtesies,
Shall not be forgot.
 Clo. Why harke you Maister; bones, what haue you done?
What, giuen away the Wench you made me take such paines
for? you are wise indeed : Masse and I had knowne of that, I
would ha e had her my selfe : fayth Maister, now we may goe
to breakfast with a Woodcock-pie.
 Seg. Goe sir, you were best leaue this knauerie.
 Kin. Come on my Lords, let's now to Court,
Where we may finish vp the ioyfullest day

F 2.   That

The Comedie
That euer hapt to a distressed King:
Were but thy Father the *Valencia* Lord,
Present in view of this combining knot.
A shout within. Enter a Messenger.
What shout was that?
Mes. My Lord, the great *Valencia* King
Newly arriued, intreates your presence.
Mu. My Father?
King A. Prepared welcomes; giue him entertainement:
A happier Planet neuer raigned then that,
Which gouernes at this houre.   *Sound.*
*Enter the King of Valencia, Anselmo, Rodrigo, Barchino, with
others, the King runnes and imbraces his Sonne.*
King V. Rise honour of my age, food to my rest:
Condemne not (mightie King of *Aragon*)
My rude behauiour, so compeld by Nature,
That manners stood vnknowledged.
King A. What we haue to recite, would tedious prooue.
By declaration; therefore in, and feast:
To morrow the performance shall explaine,
What Words conceale; till then, Drummes speake, Belles ring,
Giue plausiue welcomes to our brother King.
Sound Drummes and Trumpets.   *Exeunt omnes.*
Enter Comedie and Enuy.
Com. How now *Enuie*? What, blushest thou alreadie?
Peepe foorth, hide not thy head with shame,
But with a courage, prayse a Womans deedes:
Thy threates were vaine, thou couldst doe me no hurt,
Although thou seemest to crosse me with despight,
I ouerwhelm'd and turned vpside downe thy blocks,
And made thy selfe to stumble at the same.
Enu. Though stumbled, yet not ouerthrowne,
Thou canst not draw my heart to mildnesse:
Yet must I needes confesse, thou hast done well,
And playd thy part, with mirth and pleasant glee:
Say all this, yet canst thou not conquere mee,
Although this time thou hast got;
Yet not the Conquest neither:

A dou

of Mucedorus.

A double Reuenge, another time Ile haue.
   Com. *Enuie,* spit thy gall,
Plot, worke, contriue; create new fallacies,
Teame from thy Wombe each minute a blacke Traytor,
Whose blood and thoughts haue twins conception :
Studie to act deedes yet vnchronicled,
Cast natiue Monsters in the moldes of Men;
Case vicious Diuels vnder sancted Rochets :
Vnhaspe the Wicket where all periureds roost,
And swarme this Ball with treasons; doe thy worst,
Thou canst not (hel-hound) crosse my steare to night,
Nor blind that glorie, where I wish delight.
   Enu. I can, I will.
   Com. Neffarious Hagge, begin,
And let vs tugge, till one the mastrie winne.
   Enu. Comedie, thou art a shallow Goose,
Ile ouerthrow thee in thine owne intent,
And make thy fall, my Comict merriment.
   Com. Thy pollicie wants grauitie; thou art too weake :
Speake Fiend, as how?
   Enu. Why thus;
From my foule Studie will I hoyst a Wretch,
A leane and hungry Neager Canniball :
Whose iawes swell to his eyes, with chawing Malice :
And him Ile make a Poet.
   Com. What's that to'th purpose?
   Enu. This scrambling Rauen, with his needie Beard,
Will I whet on to write a Comedie,
Wherein shall be compos'd darke sentences,
Pleasing to factious braines.
And euery other where, place me a Iest,
Whose high abuse, shall more torment then blowes :
Then I my selfe (quicker then Lightning)
Will flie me to a puisant Magistrate,
And waighting with a Trencher, at his backe,
In midst of iollitie, rehearse those gaules,
(With some additions) so lately vented in your Theater :
He vpon this, cannot but make complaint,

The Comedie

To your great danger, or at least restraint.
   Com. Ha,ha,ha, I laugh to heare thy folly;
This is a trap for Boyes, not Men, nor such,
Especially desertfull in their doinges,
Whose stay'd discretion, rules their purposes.
I and my faction, doe eschew those vices:
But see, O see, the weary Sunne for rest
Hath laine his golden compasse to the West,
Where he perpetuall bide, and euer shine,
As *Danaus* of-spring, in his happy Clime.
Stoope *Enuie* stoope, bow to the Earth with mee,
Lets begge our Pardons on our bended knee.   *They kneele.*
   Enu. My Power hath lost her Might; *Enuies* date's expired.
Yon splendant Maiestie hath seld my sting,
And I amazed am.   *Fall downe and quake.*
   Com. Glorious and wise Arch-*Cæsar* on this earth,
At whose appearance, *Enuie's* stroken dumbe,
And all bad thinges, cease operation;
Vouchsafe to pardon our vnwilling errour,
So late presented to your Gracious view,
And weele endeuour with excesse of paine,
To please your senses in a choyser straine.
Thus we commit you to the armes of Night;
Whose spangled carkasse, would for your delight,
Striue to excell the Day; be blessed then:
Who other wishes, let him neuer speake.
   Enu. Amen,
To Fame and Honour we commend your rest;
Liue still more happie, euery houre more blest.

FINIS.

www.ingramcontent.com/pod-product-compliance
Lightning Source LLC
Chambersburg PA
CBHW061247060425
24668CB00014B/1313